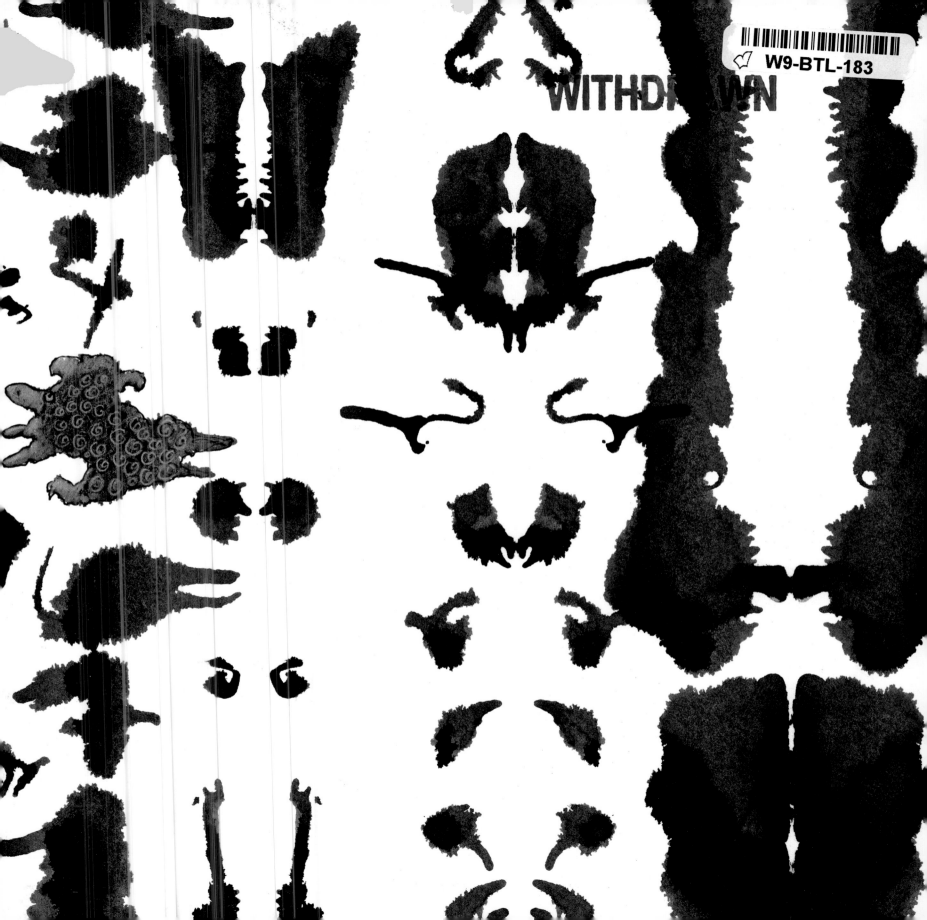

Inkblot

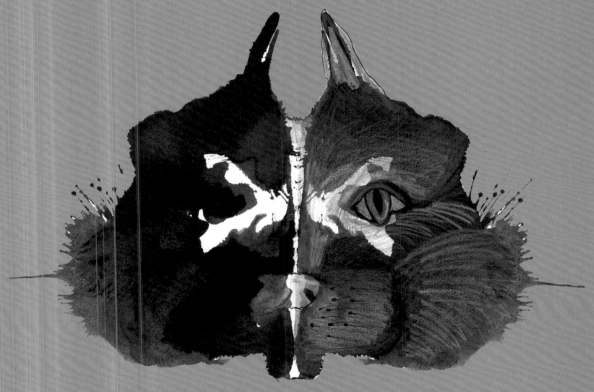

Drip, Splat, and Squish
Your Way to Creativity

Margaret Peot

BOYDS MILLS PRESS ☀ Honesdale, Pennsylvania

For Hans and Kathie Peot

Credits
Illustrations: All were created by the author, with the following exceptions: pages 20
(bottom) and 21: Victor Hugo, The Art Gallery Collection/Alamy; page 23: Stefan G.
Bucher; page 45 (lower right): Justinus Kerner; pages 50–55: various artists, as credited.
Photographs: pages 32–33: Lars Klove; pages 40–41, 44, and 47: Guy Cali Associates, Inc.
Text: page 3: Da Vinci, Leonardo. *Treatise on Painting*. London: George Bell and Sons, 1877;
page 21: Daudet, Léon. *Le Voyage de Shakespeare*. Paris: Bibliothéque-Charpentier, 1896.
Translated by Carol Wallace.

Design by Carla Weise.

www.theinkblotbook.com

Boyds Mills Press, Inc.
815 Church Street
Honesdale, Pennsylvania 18431
Printed in the United States of America

ISBN: 978-1-59078-720-5

Library of Congress Control Number: 2010929541

First edition
The text of this book is set in Calisto MT.

10 9 8 7 6 5 4 3 2 1

By looking attentively at old and smeared walls, or stones and veined marble of various colors, you may fancy that you see in them several compositions, landscapes, battles, figures in quick motion, strange countenances, and dresses, with an infinity of other objects. By these confused lines, the inventive genius is excited to new exertions.

—LEONARDO DA VINCI, *TREATISE ON PAINTING*

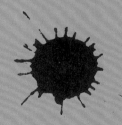

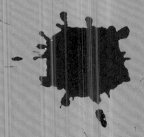

Acknowledgments

Books begin and come to fruition with the support of family, friends, and teachers: Sam and Daniel Levy, who made many inkblots along with me; my mother, who saved my first inkblot book for more than thirty years, giving me the seeds of the idea for this one; Ardis Macaulay, who got me started drawing into inkblots when I was a teenager.

Robin Glazer at The Creative Center offered me the opportunity to teach inkblot workshops to cancer survivors. Stefan G. Bucher inspired me with his wonderful ink monsters. Thanks to Lars Klove for the specimen box photograph and to Carol Wallace, who found and translated the wonderful quote from Léon Daudet.

I would like to thank my editor, Andy Boyles, for his creativity and humor, and my agent, Anna Olswanger, for her care and enthusiasm.

Finally, a heartfelt thanks to the Inkblot Gallery artists and their parents.

Contents

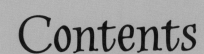

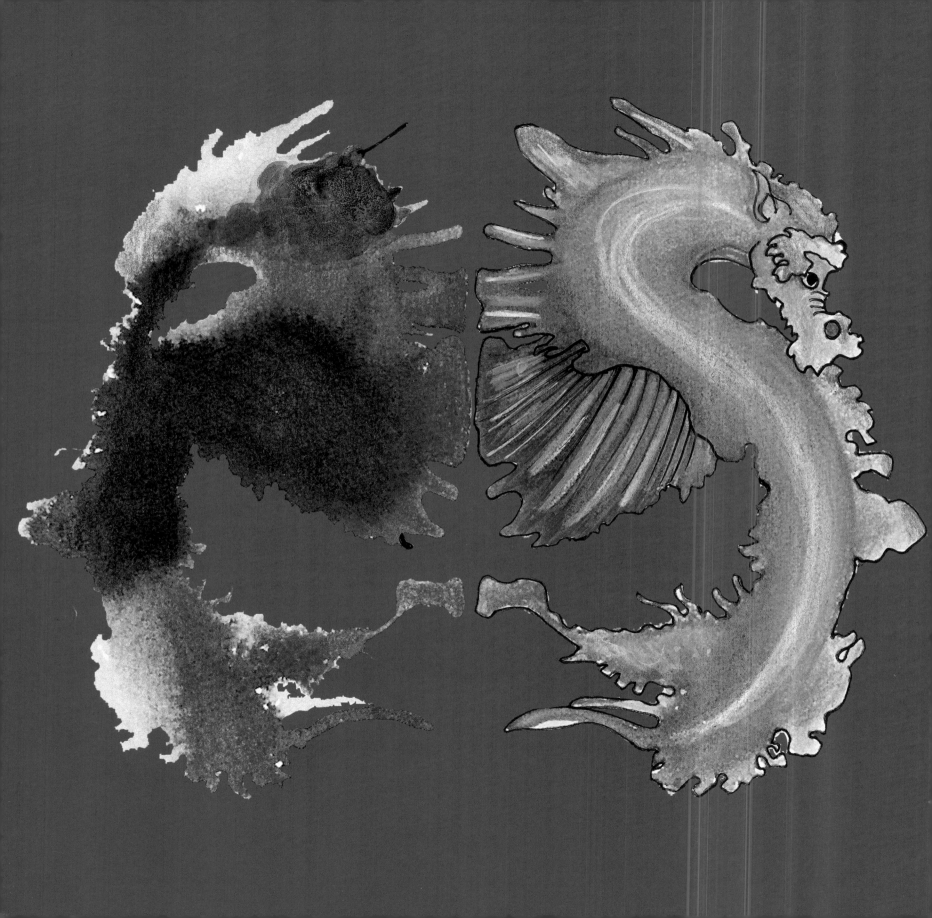

Introduction

How often have you sat waiting for creativity to strike? An important report is due or you need an idea for the backdrop in a play or an important multimedia presentation remains unstarted. And nothing is coming to you.

Scientists who study the brain have found that the right side, or hemisphere, of the brain is the side that governs creativity and intuition, and that the left hemisphere handles logical analysis of information and collection of data. Some people are more right-brained, or intuitive, and others are more left-brained, or analytical. To be an effective, and perhaps *extraordinary*, problem solver, you need to use both sides of your brain efficiently.

A powerful way to tap into your creativity, using both your intuitive and your analytical halves, is through inkblots.

The Appeal of Inkblots

Inkblots are simply dried ink and water on paper. They have no concrete form, and yet looking at them neatly sidesteps our critical left brain to evoke words, images, and stories.

Like snowflakes—and people, too—no two inkblots are alike. And yet inkblots are always distinctly and inexplicably like the people who make them, despite the seemingly random method we use to generate them.

Throughout this book, you will discover that inkblots are tools for overcoming creative blocks, for inspiring ideas, and for opening up avenues for creative expression. Anyone can use this fun and fascinating method to jump-start creative thought.

Creativity

Some people seem to be more creative than others. What is their secret? Many creative people say that it is important to *cultivate playfulness* and to do so *regularly*.

Daily life is rich in experiences that exercise the analytical, not-so-creative left brain—wake up on time, gather everything you will need for the day, solve the problems, memorize the facts, and so on. Scheduling idle time to play, write, dance, sing, or draw gives your right brain a turn.

Creative people do not wait around for their muses to show up. They go to their drawing boards (or computers or laboratories) on a daily basis, whether or not they have an idea. When your body and mind get in a habit of being creative on a schedule, you are much less likely to be creatively blocked.

When you start working with inkblots, you will find yourself seeing the whole world differently—every day!

Art Materials and Supplies

The following is a list of the basic supplies that you will need for most of the projects in this book. Others are listed as needed.

* Lightweight or medium-weight paper, such as drawing paper, printmaking paper, or computer paper. Some projects call for large sheets, such as 18" x 24" or 22" x 30".
* Tracing paper
* India ink. I recommend a small bottle, with dropper. Tip: India ink is permanent. Wear old clothes or an apron when making inkblots.
* Colored inks
* Water in a small squeeze bottle
* Eyedroppers
* Small brush or cotton swabs
* Drafting compass
* Shallow basin for ink and water, such as a lid or Styrofoam tray
* Rubber gloves
* Drinking straws
* Black pen, such as a roller-ball or felt-tip. Sakura Pigma Micron, Pilot (acid-free gel), Zebra Sarasa, and Faber-Castell PITT Artist are all suitable brands.
* Colored pencils or crayons. China markers (grease pencils), Prismacolor, or some other brand of highly pigmented colored pencil or crayon will cover the ink well.

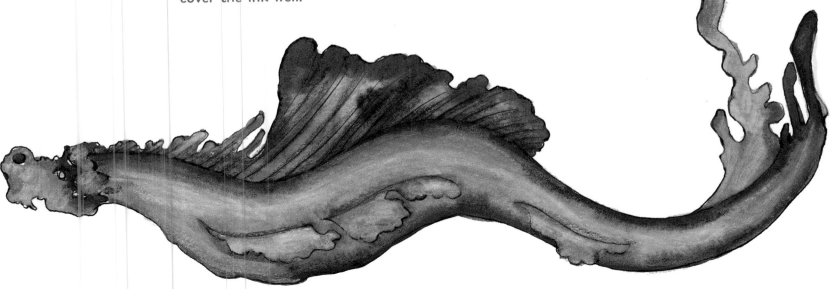

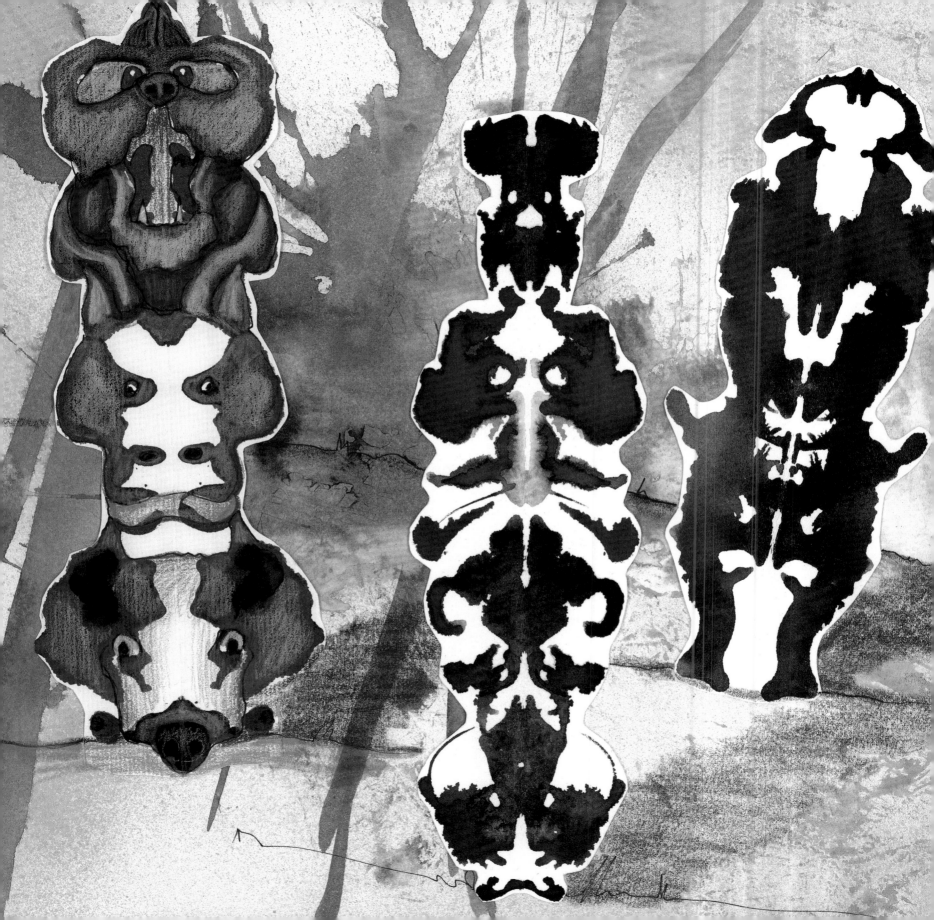

1

Making
Inkblots

HOW TO BEGIN

What Is an Inkblot?

An inkblot is a blob, smudge, drip, or fleck of ink on a piece of paper. The traditional inkblot of Rorschach fame is a blob of ink on paper that is then folded on itself and unfolded to make a bilaterally symmetrical image. We can make other kinds of inkblots by blobbing the ink and then folding the paper onto the ink multiple times, by pouring ink and swirling it around, or by dripping ink on a page on the floor from waist height.

Single-Fold Inkblot

No particular artistic skill is required to make a beautiful inkblot. You will find that the weight and type of paper you use will vary the appearance of your blots. Some printmaking papers make bold, simple inkblots; drawing papers make more detailed inkblots. The differences among the papers and the inkblots they make have to do with the amount of sizing, or binder, in each paper. The more sizing, the less absorbent the paper.

You will need:

* ❈ Four to eight pieces of medium-weight art paper, 10″ x 15″ or smaller
* ❈ India ink
* ❈ Water
* ❈ Eyedropper
* ❈ Small brush or cotton swabs

HOW TO DO IT

Three Ways to Shape and Trim Paper

SCISSORS: Scissors are ideal if you need to cut paper into a shape that has no straight edges—a circle, for example.

GUILLOTINE PAPER CUTTER: For neat, straight edges, you can use this tool. Ask an adult to show you how to use it safely.

TEARING: Artists often divide paper into smaller sheets by tearing it. This is because most art paper has softly feathered (or deckle) edges. Cutting makes a blunt edge, but tearing leaves an edge that mimics the deckle edge. To tear paper, fold it, then run a table knife (not too sharp) along the inside of the crease to separate the paper at the fold. Or lay a metal ruler along the line and pull the paper up and slightly over the ruler to tear it against the metal edge.

Hermann Rorschach

Hermann Rorschach (1884–1922) developed an inkblot test to use in psychoanalysis. He believed that what people saw in inkblots could give him a window into their subconscious. His approach is still widely used.

The Rorschach Test had its origins in the game Blotto, which was popular in Europe during the late 1800s and early 1900s. Using cards that showed a variety of inkblots, players would write poems based on the blots or compete in describing the blots in great detail.

Hermann Rorschach played Blotto (or *Klecksographie*, as it was known in German, *klecks* meaning *inkblot*) into adulthood and became increasingly fascinated by the similarities and differences in the descriptions given by the players. In fact, Rorschach's nickname among his friends was Klecks. Eventually, he developed ten different inkblots, five black-and-gray and five in color—the now-famous Rorschach Test.

Apply ink to a piece of paper using the dropper, brush, or cotton swab. You won't need a lot—just a couple of drops or swirls. Add a drop or two of water. Fold the inked paper in half and press the halves together. Unfold. Let dry. Make another. It will take a few tries to get the hang of how much ink and water to use.

Application of ink before folding

Dab ink. Drop ink. Splat ink. Make puddles and lines and swirls and crisscrosses. Try putting ink right in the middle of the paper before folding. On another, add ink only around the edges of the paper, avoiding the middle. If you are not satisfied with the way your inkblot looks, you can add another dot or so of ink and fold again. If your inkblot has gotten too wet, let it dry before adding more ink.

HOW TO DO IT

The Pressure Is On!

How you apply pressure to the inked, folded paper will change the appearance of your inkblot. Try these techniques:

1. Press straight down with the full flat of your palm.
2. Press lightly.
3. Press heavily and firmly.
4. Apply pressure with one finger moving in a spiral over the folded paper.
5. Apply pressure moving outward from the fold.
6. Apply pressure with your fingers from the edges of the paper toward the fold.
7. Slam the halves of the paper together.

A "slammed" effect

Colored Ink

Try using colored ink to make inkblots, or use it along with the India ink. Several kinds of colored ink are available in art-supply and craft-supply stores.

Using colored inks, you can build up a rich surface by adding different colors and folding multiple times. It might look like mud when it is wet, but when it dries, you may find some surprising color effects.

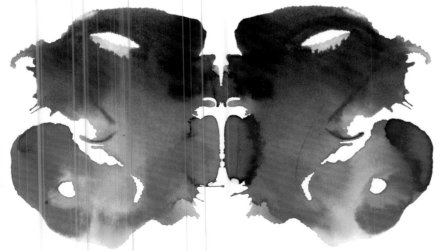

HOW TO DO IT

Pre-folding

For best results, fold your paper before applying ink and water.

If you ink and then fold, the ink ends up squirting out the top and bottom of the fold of the paper. If you fold first, then add ink, the ink will stay in place and you will have more control of your technique. You can gently press the sides of the paper together or slam the middle of the paper with the palm of your hand or gently smooth the halves together.

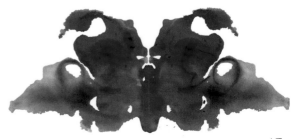

Fantastic Planets, Mysterious Worlds

Circular Inkblots

You can make circular inkblots by dropping ink and water within a compass-drawn circle and applying pressure around the perimeter of the circle after folding the paper.

You will need:

- ☀ Large sheets of medium-weight paper
- ☀ Drafting compass
- ☀ India ink or colored ink
- ☀ Water

Pre-fold the paper. On the approximate center of the fold line, use a compass to draw a circle that fits within the edges of the paper, or trace a circle using a round object such as a plate or lid.

The line you draw indicates the outer perimeter of your circular inkblot. Drip a little ink and a little water inside the circle, and gently fold. When you press down, move the palm of your hand gently toward the fold line, the center of the circle. Unfold the paper and look at the blot. Add more ink if you want—maybe even a thin bead of ink around the edge of the circle—then fold and press toward the center again. Keep adding ink and refolding until the circle is filled in to your satisfaction. If the paper starts to become mushy, let the blot dry before you add more ink.

If a few ink blobs escape the circle, that's fine. Think of them as solar flares, space stations, or perhaps giant aliens visiting from other worlds!

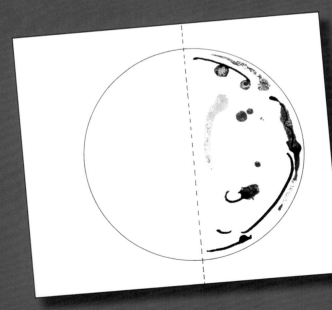

Application of ink before folding

Inkblot Variations

Long, thin inkblots, multifold blots, poured inkblots, inkblot "landscapes," and blown inkblots each require a specific technique. You may discover new methods as you become familiar with the materials. Your personality will determine whether you slop on the ink with abandon or put it on carefully, shrewdly, with a grand plan in mind.

Long, Thin Inkblots

You can create an inkblot of any shape and size by changing the way you apply ink and pressure. A long, thin, vertical inkblot can look like a rocket, a tree, or a person. If you turn it horizontally, you may see an inky landscape—trees, bushes, and hidden creatures reflected in a smooth river.

Pre-fold your paper. Apply a small amount of ink and water close to and all along the fold. Fold gently, using your finger to press toward the fold and up and down along the fold. Add a bit more ink if you wish, and refold the paper.

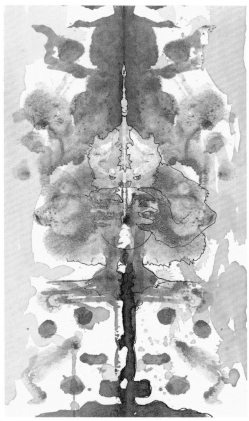

You will need:

- ❋ Lightweight paper
- ❋ India ink
- ❋ Colored ink
- ❋ Water

17

Multifold Inkblots

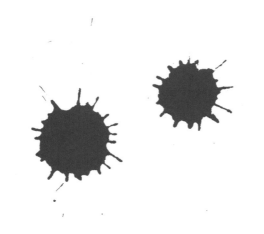

When you apply ink and water to a piece of lightweight paper and fold it more than once, you can make ornate inkblots—inkblots that look like chandeliers, flowers, or mandalas.

You will need:

- ☼ Lightweight paper
- ☼ India ink
- ☼ Colored ink
- ☼ Water

Tear your paper into approximate squares (see HOW TO DO IT: Three Ways to Shape and Trim Paper, page 13).

Two Folds

Pre-fold your paper before applying ink. Fold your paper in half, then in half again, with the second fold perpendicular to the first. Unfold the paper. Apply a little ink and water, and fold the paper one way and unfold. Without adding more ink, fold along the other fold. After making a couple of inkblots, you will develop a feel for how much ink to use.

Four Folds

Pre-fold your paper, as above, and add two more folds, diagonally, from corner to corner. Add ink and water and fold along each of the four folds, one at a time. Depending on the kind of paper, you might have to add a little more ink and moisture when you get to the third and fourth folds.

Landscapes

You will need:

- ※ Medium-weight paper
- ※ India ink
- ※ Colored ink
- ※ Water
- ※ Shallow tray
- ※ Natural materials, such as weeds, interesting dried grasses that have a seed-fluff on the top, or a twig with a few leaves attached

Lay a piece of the natural material in the shallow tray, and pour a little ink and water directly on it. You won't need a lot. Slosh the stems or leaves around in the ink and water until they are somewhat saturated.

Pre-fold a piece of paper and lay the inky natural material on it. Fold, pressing the paper down. Feel gently through the paper to press along the contours of the stems or leaves. Unfold and remove the plant matter.

Let this dry, and if you wish, add ink and water in drops to the paper and make a blot behind your plant image, perhaps with colored ink.

How could you change or enhance your inkblot landscape by drawing into it? Could you add a castle? An insect? Let the scale of the landscape change in your mind as you consider these additions. We'll go further into this kind of exploration in chapter 3.

Victor Hugo

Victor Hugo was a writer in France in the mid-1800s. He is perhaps most famous for his novels *Les Misérables* and *The Hunchback of Notre Dame*. Hugo was also an accomplished artist. He often used his drawings to inspire his written work, sometimes starting a drawing in the middle of his writing, using the same quill pen. Perhaps this was why ink on paper was his medium of choice.

He used single-fold inkblots, multifold inkblots, and ink pouring as ways to start his artworks, drawing into them to create ghostly castles, strange creatures, and haunting landscapes.

He had a unique and improbable working method, one that can teach everyone. He would toss onto a piece of paper some wine, some ink, some plum juice, sometimes some blood when he had pricked a vein. Then he would spend a long time considering the outline of these spatters, and as there is no chaos that the human gaze does not humanize, he would discover fortified castles and fountains, lions fighting, hydras, fantastic forests, an entire dream architecture, powerfully lit and shadowed. . . . This manner of creation placed him in the category of the monstrous. Horror is his domain. . . .

—Novelist Léon Daudet, describing a fictional character based on his wife's grandfather, Victor Hugo

Ink Pouring

The famous author Victor Hugo didn't always fold his blots to make symmetrical prints. Sometimes he used a mixture of coffee and ink or wine to create wonderful textures, mysterious forests, dark swamps, and creepy flora.

You will need:

- ☀ Lightweight paper or card stock. For this exercise, avoid using paper that is too thin, like computer paper, since you will be picking it up while it is wet.
- ☀ India ink
- ☀ Colored ink
- ☀ Water

Drop ink and water on a piece of paper. Instead of folding it, hold the paper on the palm of your hand and tip it in different directions as if you were a waiter bobbling and balancing a tray. The inks will travel around and mix with one another and with the water to make an interesting picture. A lot of the ink will drip off the edges of the paper. When you have a picture you like, lay it carefully on a piece of newspaper to dry. The puddles of ink will be beautiful when they dry, glistening like mineral deposits on the edge of a gold-rush stream.

Blown Ink

If you drop ink onto a page and blow air through a straw at the wet puddle, you will get the most remarkable tendrils, winter branches, spiky hair, strange grasses, elongated mushrooms, and other fantastic shapes.

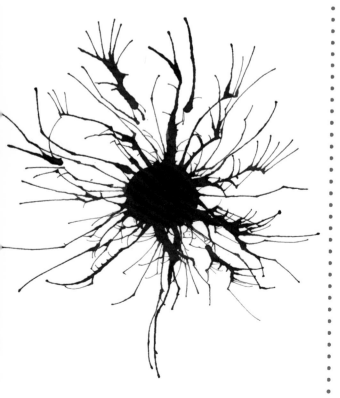

Stefan G. Bucher

The master of the blown-ink technique, without question, is Stefan G. Bucher. The book *100 Days of Monsters: From the Twisted Mind of Stefan G. Bucher and his Band of Authors at Dailymonster.com* is a fantastic collection of blown inkblots that have been transformed into monsters by Stefan and then commented on by his legion of followers. Stefan filmed his hand as he drew one hundred inkblot monsters in one hundred days and then posted his drawings on his Web site, www.dailymonster.com.

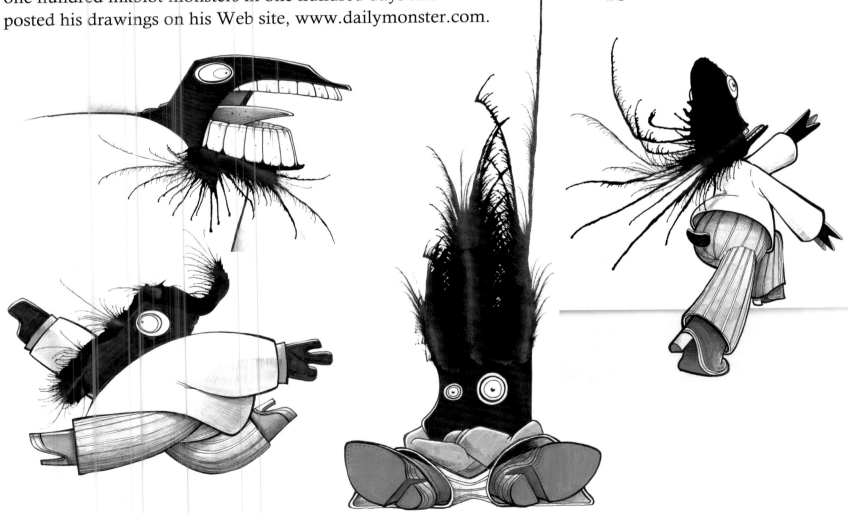

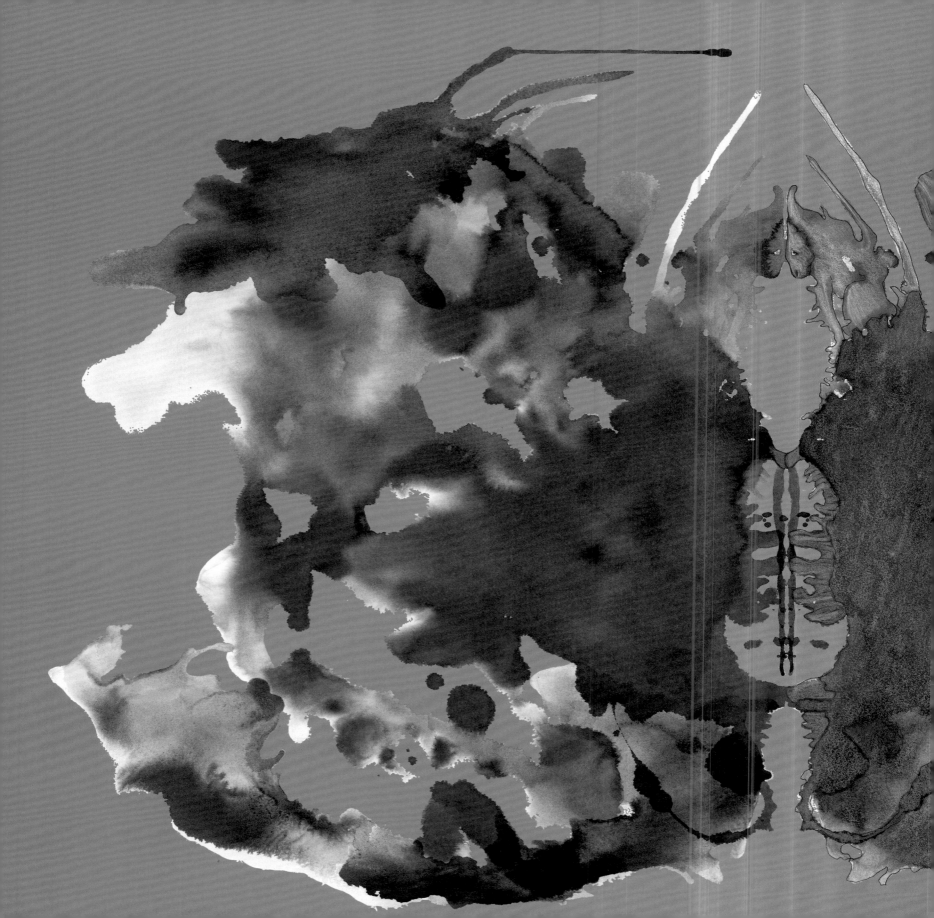

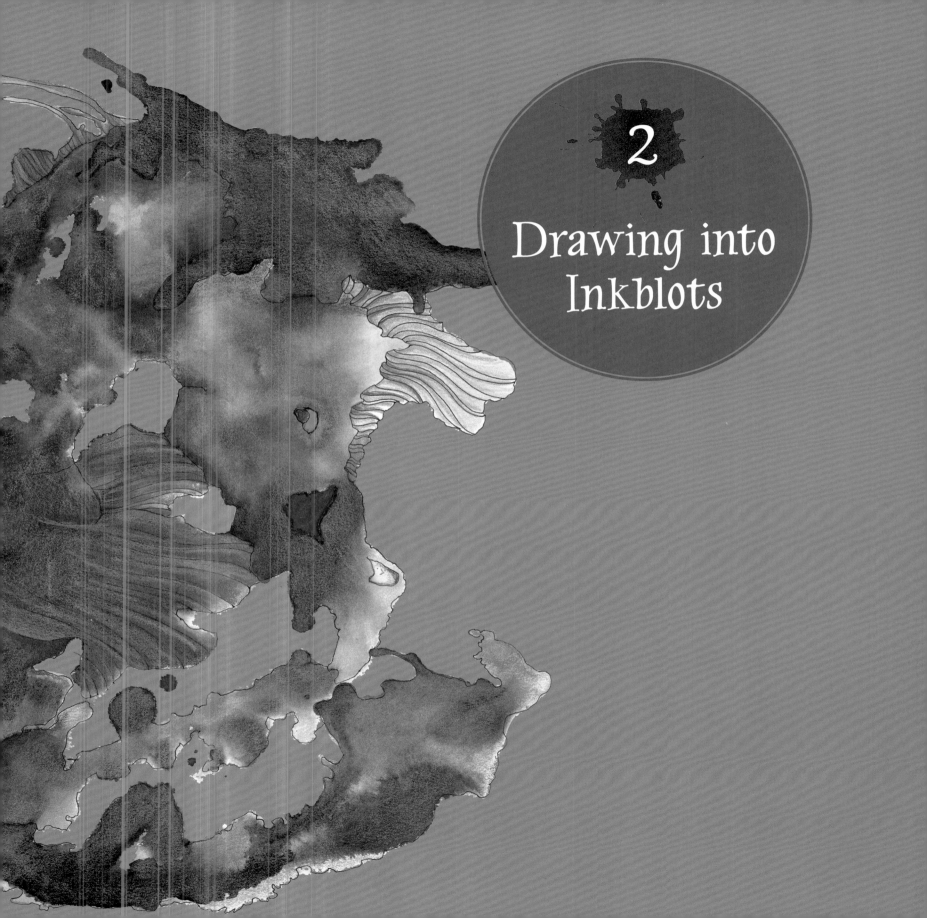

2

Drawing into Inkblots

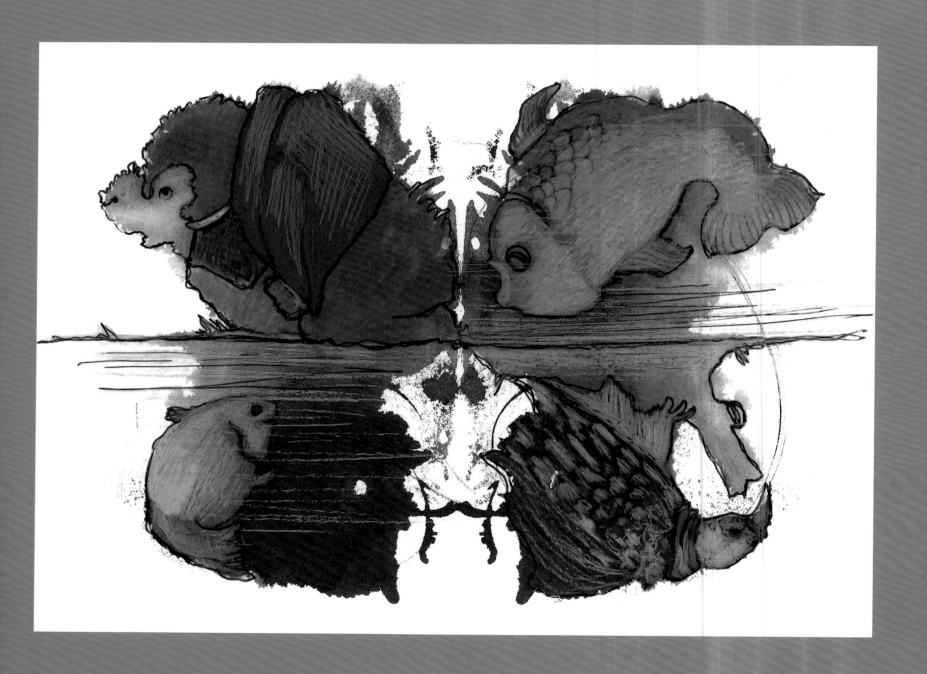

ADDING LINES AND COLORS

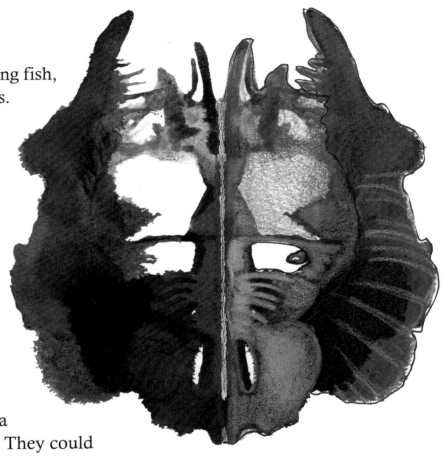

rrange inkblots around you. You might see kissing fish,
sailing ships, faces, flowers, planets, or monsters.
There could be a tornado, a volcano, or a maelstrom.
You might see a spaceship ready to take you on a
wonderful planetary adventure to meet the denizens
of that world and explore its flora and fauna. What
you see in your inkblots will be as individual as you
are, and best of all, there are no wrong answers! The
possibilities in inkblots, and the potential for creative
interpretation, are limitless.

In this chapter you will find tips for drawing
into inkblots as well as some tracing-paper tricks to
prepare your brain for ultimate creativity!

Drawing into an inkblot is as simple as drawing
around what you see in the blot, and then coloring
it in. That's it. Some people might see a creature in a
landscape or a vase of flowers—a complete picture. They could
draw around all of the elements and color them in, leaving no
undrawn ink blobs behind. But more often than not, you will see
some elements that look like something, and others that do not.
If the entire inkblot doesn't speak to you, but you see a tiny duck
on one edge, then draw around the duck, color it in, and see what
develops. Maybe after you draw the duck, the rest of the inkblot
will start to look like a pond, or a mother duck, or clouds into
which the duck is gazing.

You might not see an object or a creature, but you may see an
abstract design of swirls and cloudy shapes that evoke color ideas.

You will need:

* Twenty or more inkblots
* Black pen
* Colored pencils or crayons

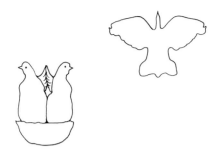

As you begin to draw into your inkblots, you will have to throw out any preconceived notions of what should go together, what creatures might meet within a picture, what they will be capable of doing. Even the law of gravity may not apply in your inkblot world.

Tracing-Paper Tricks

You might want to do a little planning before you start drawing into your inkblots. Lay the inkblots you have made around you, and use the questions on the next page as well as tracing paper and a pencil to get you going. Try thinking of your inkblots as puzzles in which you have to find the hidden images.

You will need:

* Inkblots
* Tracing paper
* Pencil or pen

These tracings show the many images the author discovered in this single inkblot.

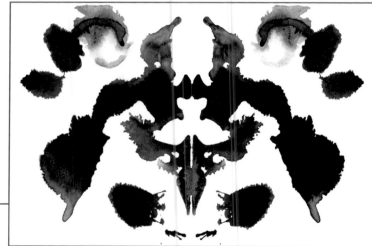

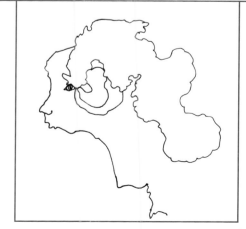

28

1. Pick an inkblot that interests you.

2. What do you see in it? What could you do to make it clearer? Lay a piece of tracing paper over the inkblot, and draw lines on the tracing paper to "enhance" the figures or images you see. If you see a face, add a neck or eyes. If you see no figures, add to the abstract image you see.

3. Lay a fresh piece of tracing paper over the inkblot. Draw lines on the tracing paper to make an environment for the figures or images you see. Do you see a planet? Draw a galaxy around it. Do you see a flower? Draw a garden.

4. Look at the negative shapes, the white spaces in and around the inked areas. Place a new piece of tracing paper over the inkblot and trace around these negative shapes. Lift the tracing paper and discover what you have drawn.

5. Even though this is a black-and-white inkblot, do any other colors come to mind while you look at it? Which color or colors?

6. In the inkblot, is anything being shared here? A confidence? A secret? A bowl? Money?

Draw into a few inkblots. It might take a while to get into the swing of seeing into them, but once you get started, it's hard to stop. The inkblots you draw into can be finished paintings as they are, or they might launch your mind into other realms. The characters, places, and shapes you find can be the beginning of anything—a story, a comic-book character, a land for you to explore, botanical specimens to collect and categorize.

Other Symmetrical Shapes

You have coaxed ink and water into circles and long, thin blots. You can make other symmetrical forms as well. A square might be tricky because it has such specifically angular qualities. Could you make a heart? How would you do it? How could you make an inkblot butterfly?

You can make a planned inkblot with any symmetrical shape: planes, people, faces, birds, fairies, beetles, or dragons. You could also make the most elaborate, tricked-out spaceship in this galaxy or any other. You could make a fleet of them!

Application of ink before folding

You will need:

※ Lightweight paper
※ India ink
※ Colored ink
※ Water

Butterflies

Cut or tear the paper into the sizes you wish to make your butterflies, and pre-fold the paper. On one side of the fold, apply a little ink and a little water in a butterfly wing shape. Maybe add a dot or two on the wing, and put a tiny bit in the fold to squish out and form the body. Fold gently, pressing the ink down uniformly with the palm of your hand, and unfold. If this doesn't look like a butterfly to you, try some more!

After your butterflies are dry, you can color them. Add antennae and legs if you wish. You can cut them out, pin them into a box, and label them with made-up names as if they were butterfly specimens that you had collected from the deepest jungle; or you can cut them out, fold them slightly, and glue them to a branch as if they had alighted there and were going to flutter off in a moment.

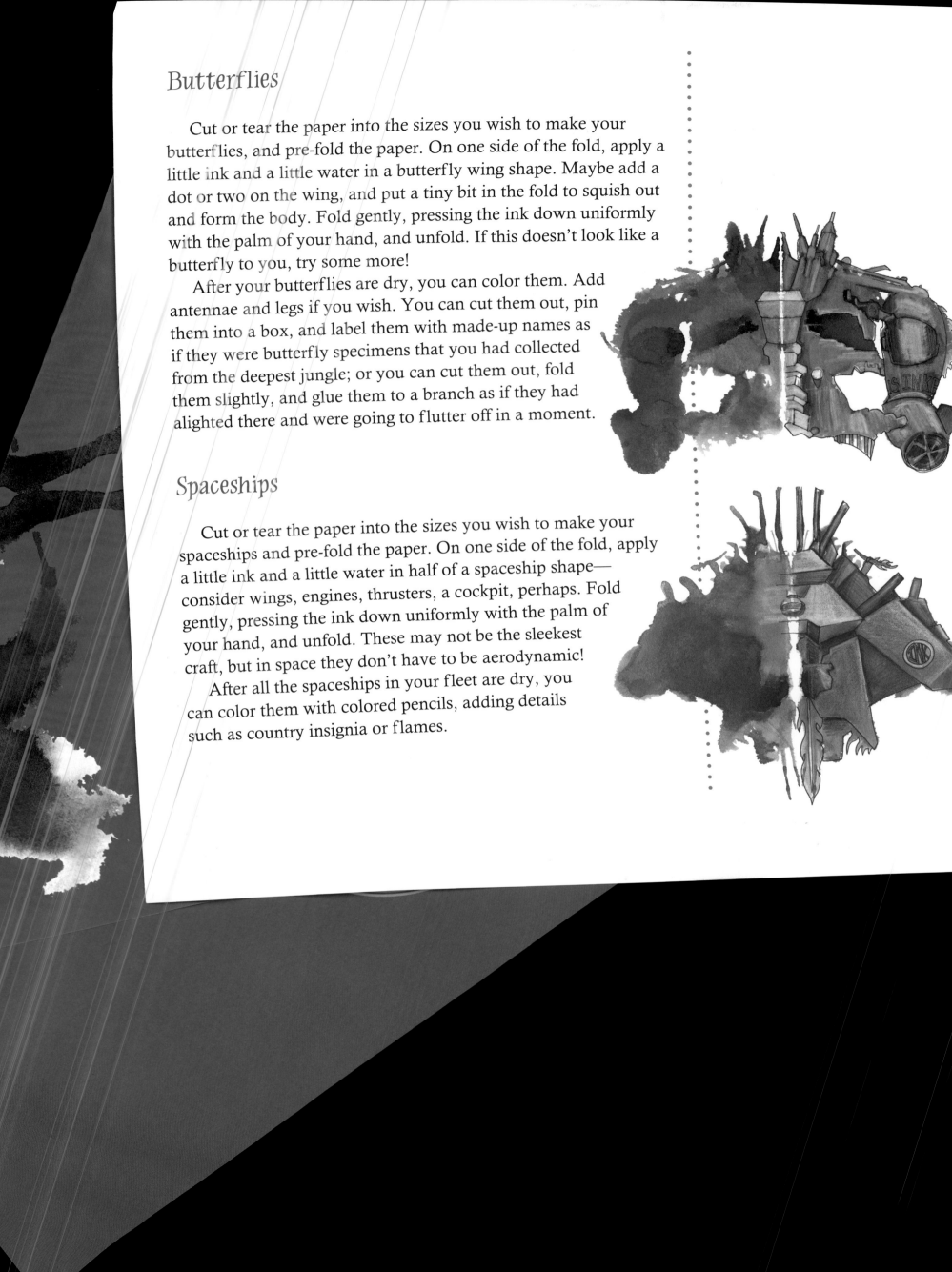

Spaceships

Cut or tear the paper into the sizes you wish to make your spaceships and pre-fold the paper. On one side of the fold, apply a little ink and a little water in half of a spaceship shape—consider wings, engines, thrusters, a cockpit, perhaps. Fold gently, pressing the ink down uniformly with the palm of your hand, and unfold. These may not be the sleekest craft, but in space they don't have to be aerodynamic!

After all the spaceships in your fleet are dry, you can color them with colored pencils, adding details such as country insignia or flames.

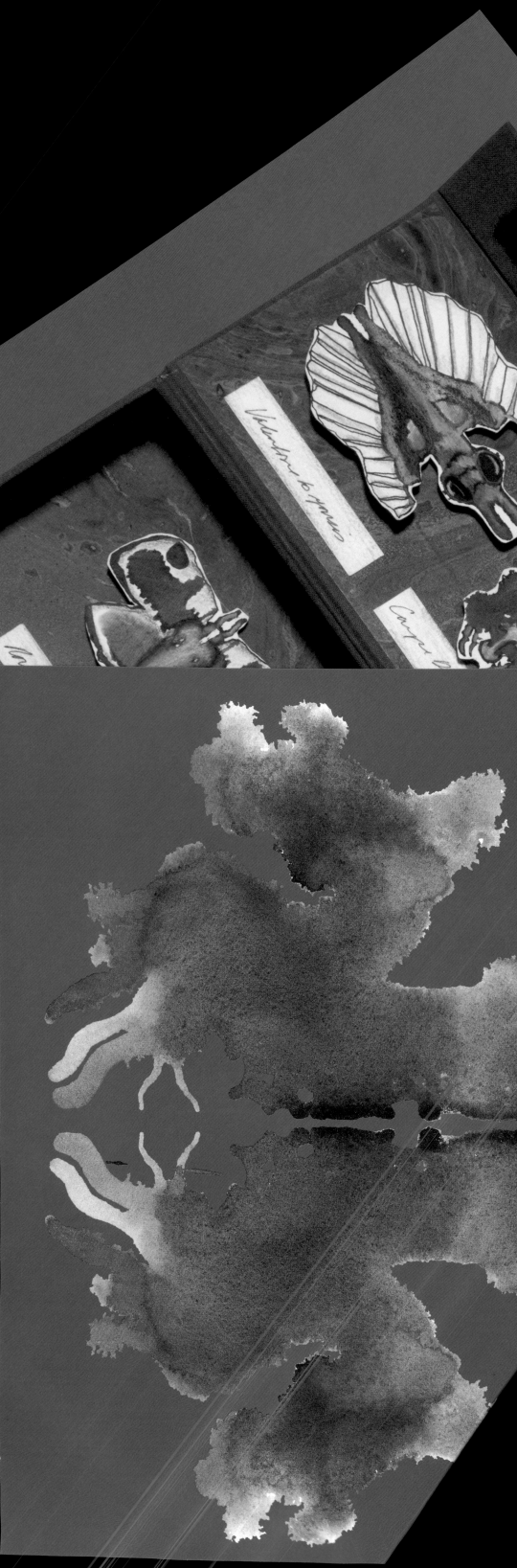

THE NEXT LEVEL OF CREATIVITY

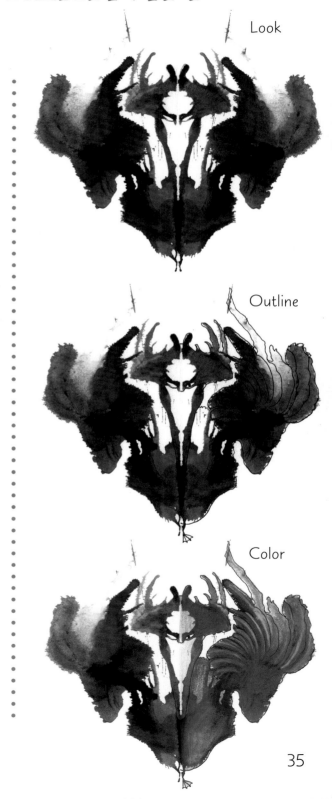

Look

Outline

Color

Have you ever looked up into a sky filled with fluffy clouds—and did you see something surprising? A puffy white pig or a writhing dragon? When we look for images in inkblots, we use the same natural urge to find meaningful patterns and shapes wherever we look.

But what can you do if you don't see anything in the inkblots you have made? In this chapter you will find techniques to stimulate your creativity.

Ten Tips for Looking at an Inkblot

1. Look at the positive shapes—the ones made by the ink and water.
2. Look at the negative shapes—the white spaces around and between the shapes made by the ink and water.
3. What is the action like in the inkblot? Is it fast and splashy? Slow and trickly?
4. Is this a heavy inkblot or a light one? Is it cloudlike or as dense as lead?
5. Is this a secret picture or a billboard for everyone to see?
6. Do you see two things side by side or facing each other or one thing facing you?
7. Where is this inkblot? Does it look as if it could be in water? In the air? Buried deep underground?
8. Is this inkblot loud or quiet?
9. Is this inkblot hot or cold?
10. Turn the inkblot upside down and try these questions again.

Silly Questions

1. You are having tea with the queen of a strange and maybe unfriendly nation. You have been served this dish (the inkblot). What are you having for tea? Is she wooing you or trying to cause an ugly international incident?

2. You are a circus impresario and need new acts for a small circus to travel the country. High-wire acts, trapeze artists, and animal acts are among those that are auditioning. Your inkblot is one of the acts auditioning for you. What is it? Do you hire it to go with your circus?

HOW TO DO IT

Sleep Tip

If you still are having trouble seeing anything in your inkblots, look at them one by one before going to bed. You might even pin or tape a few on the wall. When you wake up in the morning, you may more easily see something there.

3. You want a pet, but you must pick a pet that will get along with your prized Persian cat, Elvira. You are at a pet store and this creature (your inkblot) has caught your eye. Do you take it home? Or do you leave it at the store?

4. A famous artist is coming to paint a mural on your wall. Your inkblot is a rough sketch he has done for your approval. What is the artist going to paint on your wall? What colors would you suggest he use to paint this subject? Or do you tell him to take his brushes and go?

5. Your family is going on a trip, and your inkblot is the travel brochure for your destination. Where is it? Do you want to go with them, or would you rather stay home?

6. Pretend the inkblots are individuals. Put together a family. Pick various family members, including extended family members and pets. What is this family like? How do they relate? Who gets along better with whom?

7. You are having a party and can invite only five people. The inkblots are possible guests. Which five would you invite? Which do you definitely *not* want to come?

8. Congratulations! You are an astronomer who has discovered a new planet. Imagine your inkblot is a picture of that planet. What will you name it? What is it like there? Is there life? If so, who or what are they? Would you like to visit this planet?

9. You are making lunch for your friends. The inkblots are plates of food. From the inkblots you have made, pick a main course, salad, soup, a dessert, and a drink. What are you serving? For what occasion?

10. Animal, vegetable, mineral? If you see a bug, plant, person, or monster, where does it live? If you see an inanimate object, what is it and where would you find it?

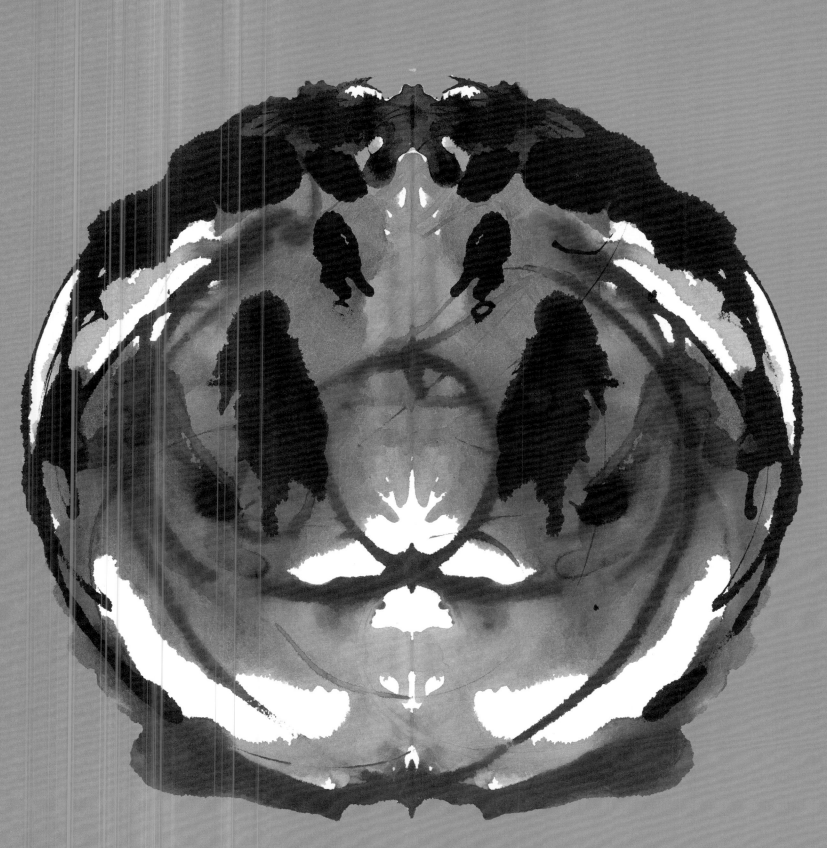

39

MY MOTHER
THE

4

The Inkblot Sketchbook

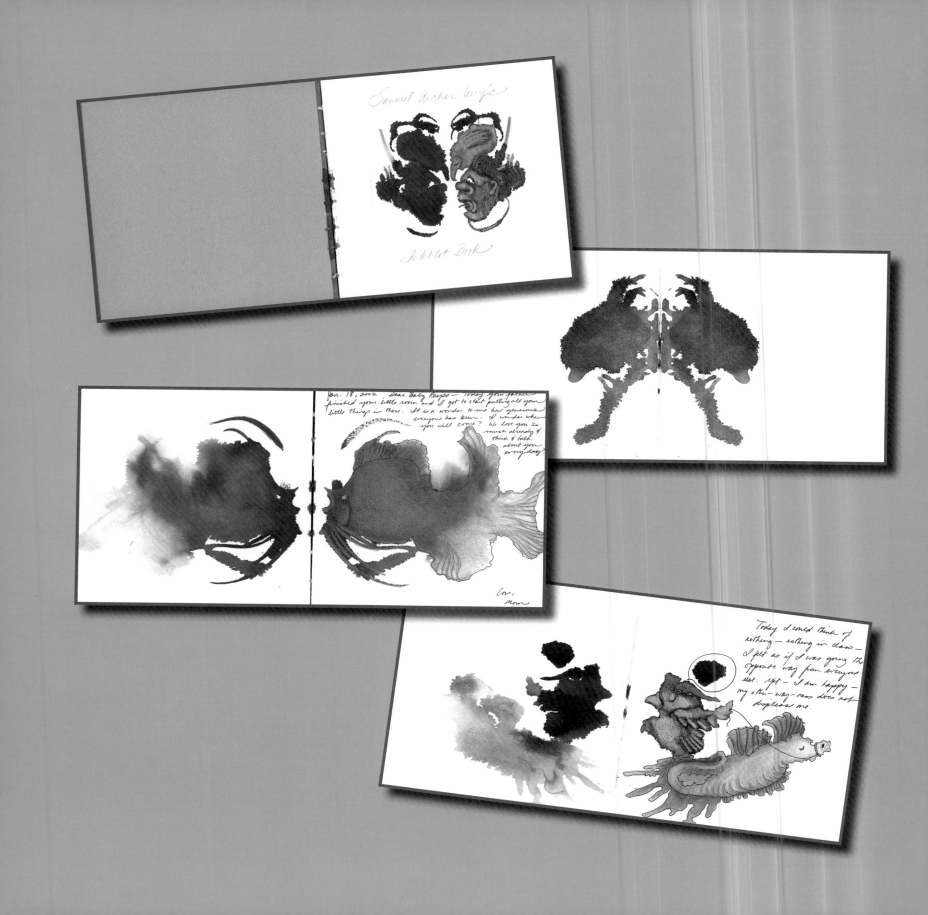

A PERSONAL PLACE TO EXPLORE

Working in a sketchbook journal on a regular basis is a great way to give your right brain consistent creative practice. And your sketchbook journal can become a destination for you: more fabulous than any television show—because it is about you, made by you—a haven, a portable art studio, a place to explore.

In this chapter, you will find tips for picking out the perfect sketchbook and how to fill your sketchbook with inkblots, as well as some fun exercises—writing and more Silly Questions—to get you started.

You will need:

- ❋ Sketchbook
- ❋ India ink
- ❋ Water
- ❋ Hair dryer (optional)

HOW TO DO IT

Four Tips for Choosing the Perfect Sketchbook

You can make your own inkblot sketchbook by creating a bunch of inkblots on plain paper and stapling them together, or you can buy an unlined sketchbook from an office-supply or art-supply store. If you are buying a sketchbook, there are some practical things to consider that may help guide your choice.

1. Size: Consider a medium-sized sketchbook that fits easily into your backpack or shoulder bag.

2. Function: The most important function of any sketchbook is that it should open easily and lie flat without a need to break the spine or weigh down the pages. Any binding style can work. Test this by holding the book open in the palm of one hand. If it stays open without help from your other hand, it's a good one.

3. Paper: Choose a sketchbook that is filled with a medium-weight, white or off-white unlined paper. You will be making inkblots in this sketchbook, so the paper in it must be sturdy enough to stand up to water. Avoid heavily textured paper, such as chunky handmade paper or rice paper with petals, twigs, and other bumpy material in it.

4. Binding: Don't choose a spiral-bound sketchbook if you are a perfectionist. The temptation to tear out pages is too great and does not honor the spirit of creativity.

Filling Your Sketchbook with Inkblots

Now you can begin filling your sketchbook with inkblots. It's going to get messy, but that's okay. It will look cool.

Follow the instructions in chapter 1 for how to make an inkblot. The place in the middle where the pages join will be the fold. Drop a little ink and water on one page, close the facing page onto the ink, press, and open. You can also fold a single page in the middle to make a smaller blot. You can either fill the book with blots or leave blank pages between blots for writing.

You will have to wait for the first batch of blots to dry before you can create more. After you make two or three inkblots, prop the book open to those pages while they dry. If you are impatient, you can dry them with a hair dryer. I suggest filling the whole book with blots before you start writing and drawing.

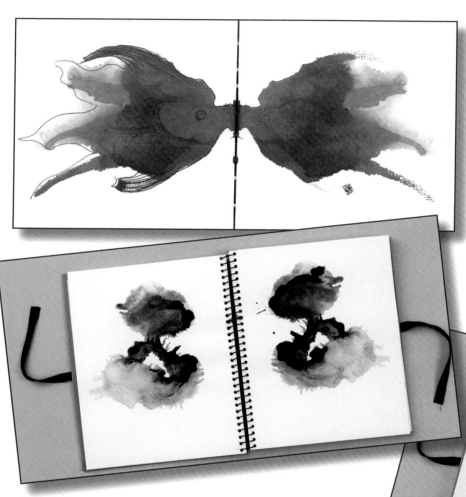

Two facing pages can form one large inkblot.

Or individual pages can be folded to make small inkblots.

THE NEGATIVE SPACE: LIKE A LITTLE
ALIEN DANCING GIRL? DANCING TOP?

TWO REINDEER-LIKE
CREATURES SITTING
ON THEIR HAUNCHES
— PLAYING PAT-A-CAKE?

PATTERNED BEETLE
WINGS, SWEPT —
LIKE A HERCULE'S
HARD WINGS?

SEALS
FLANK THE
DEER, SITTING
AT
ATTENTION

CRABS — CLAWS?

THE ROCK ON WHICH
THE REINDEER SIT

A HEDGEHOG WITH A LONG TAIL?
OSTRICH HEADS?

TURN IT UPSIDE-DOWN
AND IT LOOKS LIKE
A CRAB, OR AN ORNATE
BEETLE POISED FOR
FLIGHT

ANTENNAE

MAY 13

TWO ANTEATER-RABBITS LOOK FOR SOMETHING
TO EAT. THEY ARE WATCHED OVER
BY A BENEVOLENT RABBIT-BAT.

ON — THE
NEGATIVE
SPACE
LOOKS
LIKE A
LUNA
MOTH, AND
THE TINY WHITE
CIRCLE IS THE
FULL MOON IN
THE DISTANCE.

OR — THE RABBIT-BAT
IS PUSHING WITH ALL HIS
MIGHT TO KEEP THE CLAWS OF
A HUGE CRAB FROM SQUISHING HIM!

BEHIND THEM — ARMS? CHEST? ROCKS?
KNOW WHAT THE BLACK SHAPES ARE
AND PURPLE FEET? YELLOW BILLS. I DON'T
THEY ARE BLUE WITH COLORFUL TOPKNOTS

IS GOOD OR EVIL
PUSHING
THEY ARE
BECAUSE
OF WHAT
I CAN'T

DISSONANCES.
FEET LIKE
THEIR LEGS AND
THE BIRDS HAVE

A SPY!
A RABBIT LISTENING —
REFLECTION IS REALLY
POOL BELOW — OR THE
FACES ARE REFLECTED IN THE
THE COVER OF DARKNESS. THEIR
SPEAKING SECRETLY TO EACH OTHER UNDER
THIS INKBLOT LOOKS LIKE TWO EXOTIC BIRDS

MAY 12

Justinus Kerner

Almost fifty years before Hermann
Rorschach began implementing his
famous inkblot test, Justinus Kerner
published *Kleksographien*, a book of
poems inspired by inkblots. Kerner,
also a physician, had produced inkblots
as we have, by dropping ink onto a
piece of paper and folding it to reveal
a somewhat symmetrical image. He
then drew into the inkblots and wrote
poems inspired by them. The book,
published in Germany in 1857, was
probably known to Rorschach.

What poems might you write in
your sketchbook?

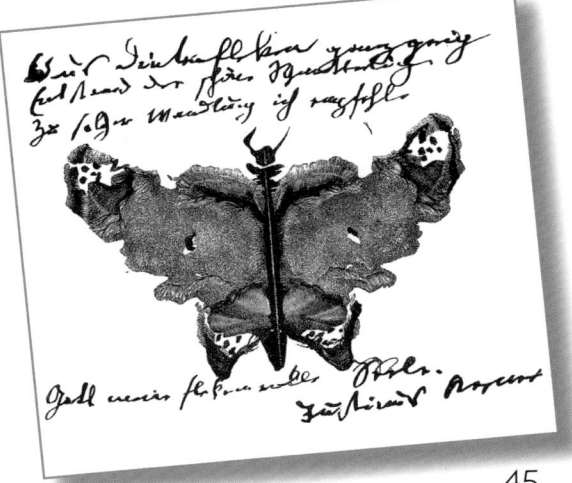

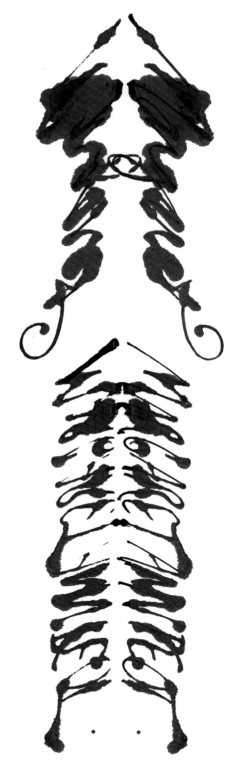

Two inkblots made from the
author's name

Jumpstart Your Writing

If you are having trouble getting started, try these jumpstart questions to get your right brain in gear. You can write either in the margins around the inkblots in your sketchbook (recommended) or on blank paper that you can fold into your book or attach in some way.

1. You are going on a trip. The inkblots in your sketchbook are travel destinations. Pick one and describe where you are going. (You are not limited to this galaxy!)
2. Make a list of things you see in the inkblot. Turn the book upside down and make a new list of the different things you see from this angle.
3. Does the inkblot image make you think of a time of year? A holiday? What makes you think so? Write down your explanation.
4. Turn to three inkblots that occur in order in your book and pretend they are illustrations for a story. In the margins or on a separate piece of paper, write the story.
5. Time machine: does the inkblot make you think of a time in history?
6. Pick an inkblot that looks creaturelike. Write about what you see and what condition it's in (neat or shabby, healthy or sick, young or old, and so on).

Signature Blots

To make signature inkblots, you'll need a pen with a nib and ink that stays wet long enough for the fold-and-press step. Most pens from an office-supply store won't work.

You will need:
- ☀ Lightweight paper
- ☀ Calligraphy pen with changeable nibs
- ☀ Small brush or cotton swabs
- ☀ India ink

Pre-fold a piece of paper. Using the calligraphy pen dipped in ink, write or print your name along the fold line. Fold and unfold. Try the same thing using a brush or cotton swab along a pre-folded line. It will take a couple of tries before you get the hang of how much ink to use to get a good signature print.

Cecil Henland thought the signature blots looked like people. What do you think?

INKBLOT HEROES

Cecil Henland and *The Ghosts of My Friends*

In the early 1900s, the children's book author Cecil Henland developed this unique autograph book, *The Ghosts of My Friends*. It is small, with smooth, pre-folded pages. She had her friends and family use an old-fashioned pen to sign their names along the fold lines and then press the other half of their pages onto the wet signatures. The friends could then draw eyes or limbs onto their signatures to heighten their human appearance, or just leave them as they were. They then signed and dated their work.

5

The Final
Fold

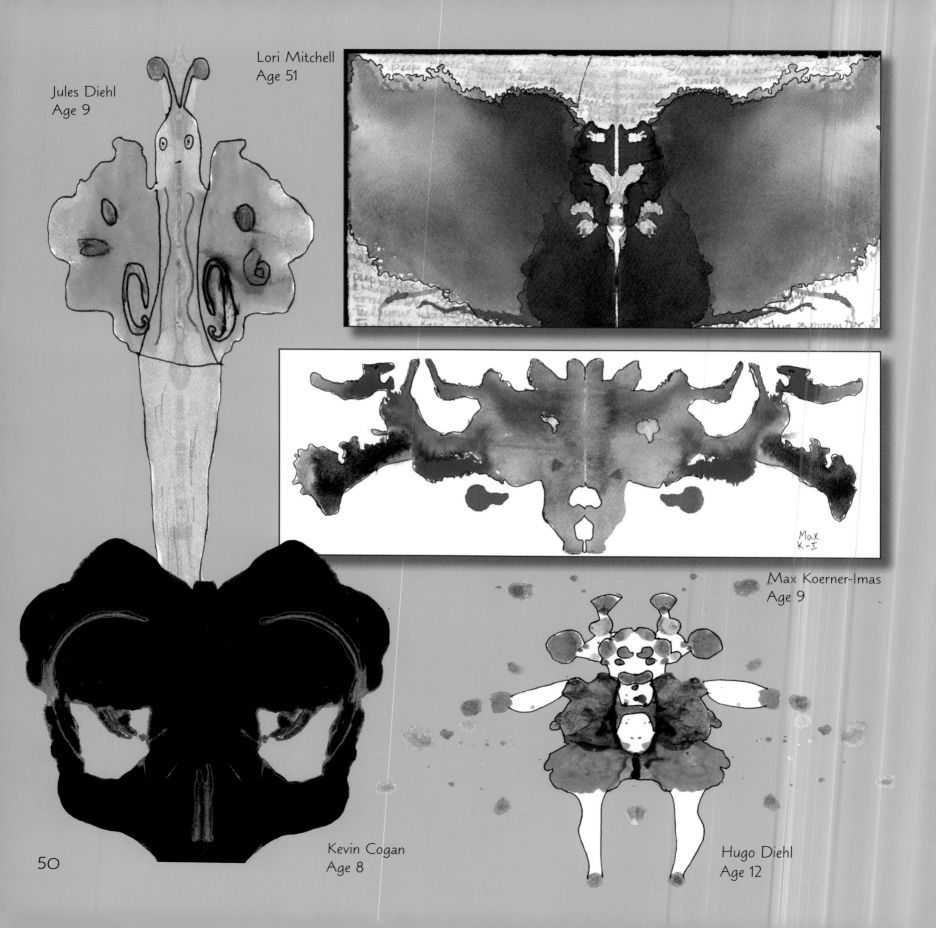

Jules Diehl
Age 9

Lori Mitchell
Age 51

Max Koerner-Imas
Age 9

Kevin Cogan
Age 8

Hugo Diehl
Age 12

50

LET YOUR JOURNEY BEGIN

Ardis Macaulay
Age 62

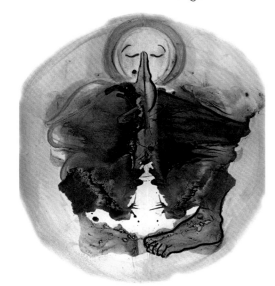

As I hope you have discovered by now, anything is possible with inkblots. You can make inkblot spaceships to go to brave new inkblot worlds, make inkblot characters on an inkblot stage, performing a play inspired by inkblots. You can be an inkblot scientist, collecting inkblot butterflies and beetles, or you can be an inkblot archaeologist, discovering inkblot artifacts on an inkblot island.

Artists have always used methods of generating random marks in an organized way to express themselves creatively and explore new ideas. Random marks—such as drips and splashes, blots, streams, and splatters—have a liveliness about them that transcends what we can imagine our hands alone doing. Victor Hugo sought out this kind of experience, as did Leonardo da Vinci, who felt inspired by random patterns in the world around him. More recently, famous artists such as Morris Louis, Andy Warhol, Jackson Pollock, Bruce Conner, Helen Frankenthaler, and countless others have used random mark-making techniques. Now you can do the same.

Let your journey begin.

Gallery of Inkblots

Here are some inkblots done by kids—and by adults who are kids at heart! For more gallery images, and to post your own inkblot work, go to my Web site, www.theinkblotbook.com.

Splat

Drip

Puddle

Drizzle

Fold

CREATE!

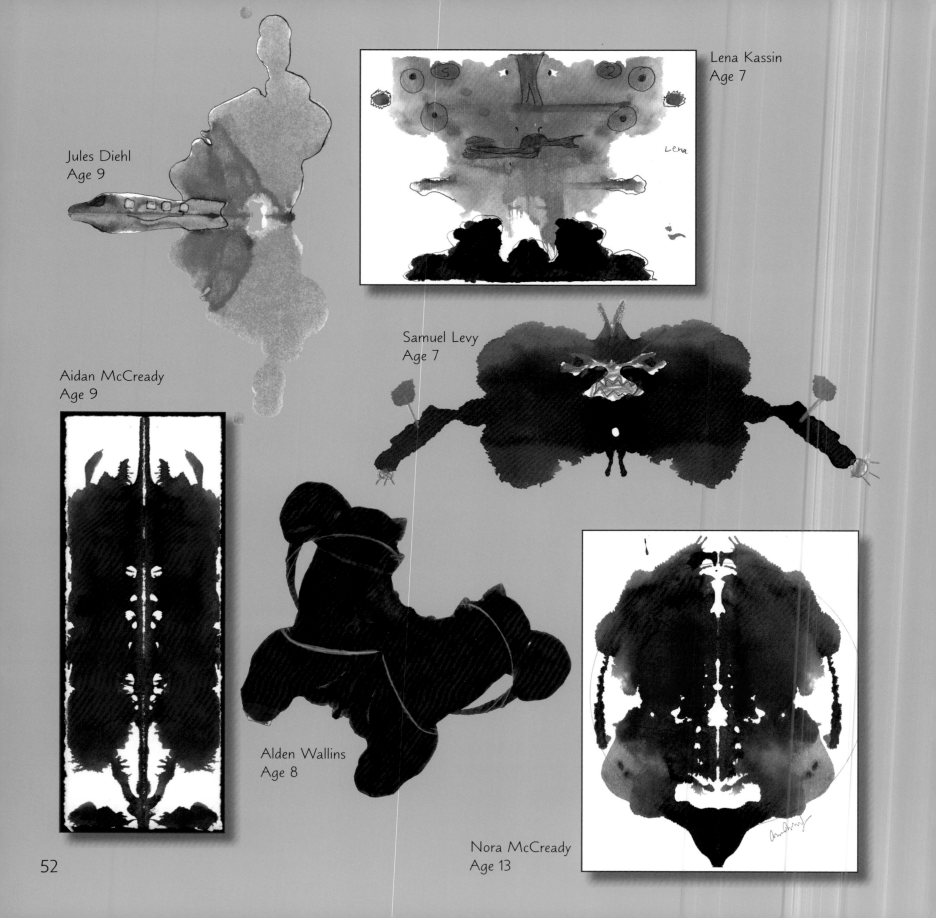

Jules Diehl
Age 9

Lena Kassin
Age 7

Samuel Levy
Age 7

Aidan McCready
Age 9

Alden Wallins
Age 8

Nora McCready
Age 13

52

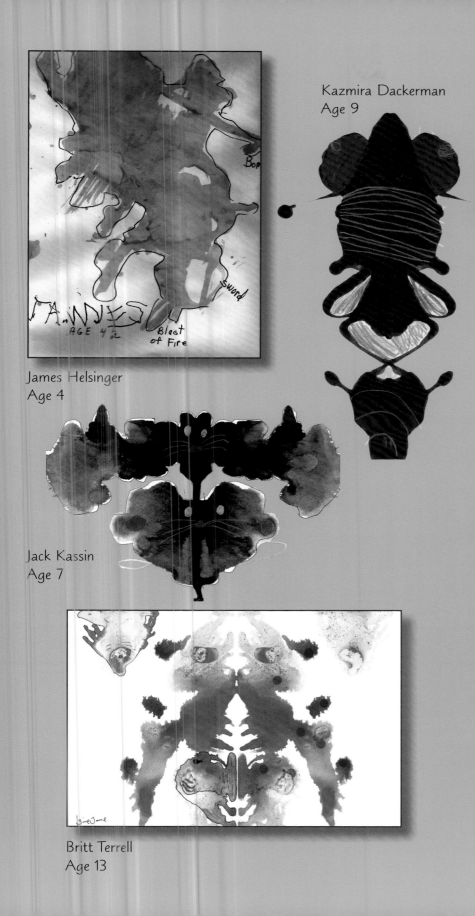

James Helsinger
Age 4

Kazmira Dackerman
Age 9

Jack Kassin
Age 7

Britt Terrell
Age 13

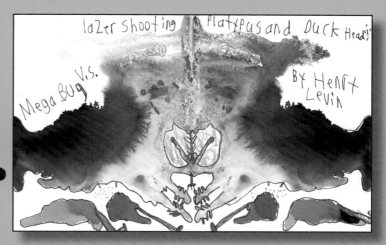

Henry Levin
Age 10

Sophie Katsivelos
Age 6

Kazmira Dackerman
Age 9

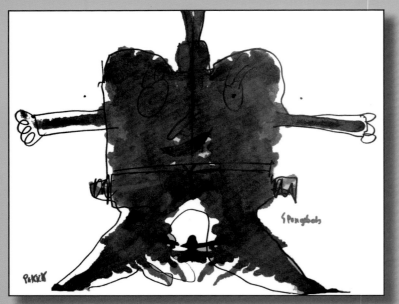

Patrick Quinn
Age 13

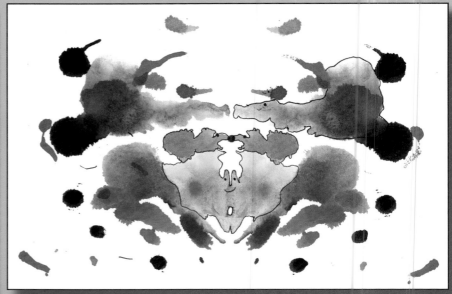

Chiara Bowker
Age 9

Rose Dallimore
Age 9

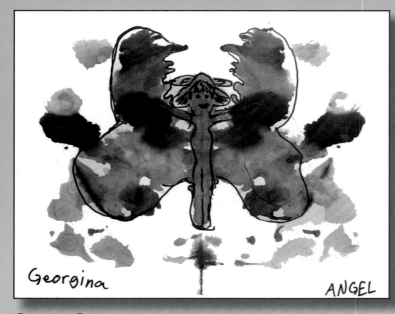

Georgina Quinn
Age 11

Nora McCready
Age 13

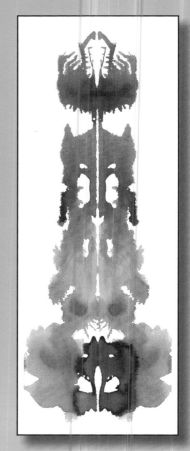

Sophie Katsivelos
Age 6

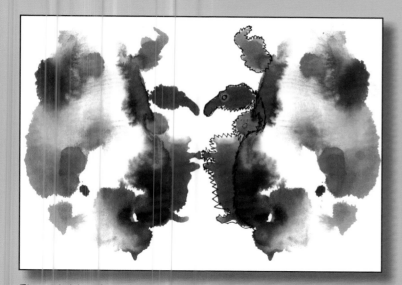

Finn Hubbard
Age 8

Grace Senoglu
Age 13

Aidan McCready
Age 9

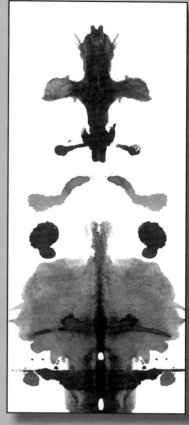

Chiara Bowker
Age 9

Samuel Levy
Age 7

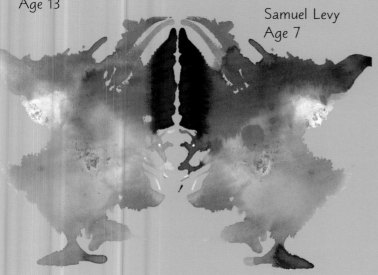

Margaret Peot
Age 5

Bibliography

Anker, Susan. "The Butterfly in the Brain." Presentation, School of Visual Arts, New York; The New York Academy of Sciences, 2009. www.nyas.org.*

Bucher, Stefan G. *100 Days of Monsters: From the Twisted Mind of Stefan G. Bucher and His Band of Authors at Dailymonster.com.* Cincinnati, OH: How Books, 2008. www.dailymonster.com.

Da Vinci, Leonardo. *Treatise on Painting.* London: George Bell and Sons, 1877.

Gaasch, Cynnie. Inkblot work in *Open Symmetry* at Gallery 164, Buffalo, NY, June 14, 2006.

Goodell, Kathy. *Mind Fields.* Wake Forest University Fine Arts Gallery, February 9–March 25, 2001. www.wfu.edu/art/gallery /mindfield.pdf.

Jackson-Forsberg, Eric. "Artshorts: 'Open' Minded." *Artvoice*, June 14, 2006. www.artvoice.com.

Kurz, Uwe. "On Chance and Coincidence in Art." The Art of Balloon-Painting. www.balloon-painting.de/ezufall.htm#kerner.

Lilienfeld, Scott O., James M. Wood, and Howard N. Garb. "What's Wrong with This Picture?" *Scientific American*, May 2001.

Peot, Margaret. *Make Your Mark: Explore Your Creativity and Discover Your Inner Artist.* San Francisco: Chronicle Books, 2004.

Rodari, Florian, Marie-Laure Prevost, Luc Sante, and Pierre Georgel. *Shadows of a Hand: The Drawings of Victor Hugo.* New York: The Drawing Center; London: Merrell Holberton, 1998.

Rosenhek, Jackie. "Inkblot Inklings: How an Artist-Cum-Scientist Dripped Ink to Paper and Projected His Way to Psychiatric Stardom." *Doctor's Review*, November 2007. www.doctorsreview.com/history /inkblot-inklings/.

Scheer, Joseph. *Night Visions: The Secret Designs of Moths.* New York: Prestel, 2003.

Shaw, Charles G. *It Looked Like Spilt Milk.* New York: HarperCollins Children's Books, 1988.

Svoboda, Elizabeth. "Faces, Faces Everywhere." *The New York Times*, February 13, 2007, Science Times, page 1.

* Web sites active at time of publication

Index